How To
LOSE
A
Custody Battle

Credits
Editors: Justin Saturley & Maggie Saturley
Photography: Maggie Saturley
Cover Design: Kylee Elizabeth

Order additional copies at
www.HowToLoseACustodyBattle.com

ISBN: 1-4392-2595-8
ISBN: 9781439225950

Library of Congress Control Number: 2009900569

Printed by CreateSpace
North Charleston, South Carolina

How To
LOSE
A
Custody Battle

by

Joseph H. Saturley, Ph.D.

<u>*Warning!!*</u>

Sense of humor required!

This book is satire.

The names and stories contained in this book are fictional.

Always consult an attorney before taking action in a legal matter.

Acknowledgements

A special thanks to my wife and soulmate, Maggie, for all you do for me and our family. Thanks to my son, Justin, for your editorial and creative input and for writing the forward to this book. Thanks to my daughter, Megan, for your patience while we pursued this task.

To my mom and dad, Geraldine and Howard Saturley, you have been wonderful parents and have taught me to put family first. To my big brothers, Jim, Tom, and Bill and to my big sister, Judy, thank you for always being there. Thanks to my brother-in-law, Tom, from whom I have learned many lessons about life in the fast lane.

Thank you to the mental health professionals, child evaluators, and my past teachers from whom I have learned much. Thank you to Bubba "The Love Sponge" Clem, whose radio show has opened the door for me to help even more families.

To the judges and attorneys I have had the pleasure of working with in the family law arena, I thank you. I have learned something from every one of you. I would like to mention many of you by name, but to do so would be to exclude others. Just know that I remember each of you and offer this acknowledgement as a specific thanks for what you have taught me.

How to Lose A Custody Battle

Table of Contents

How to Lose A Custody Battle

Foreword

Self-help books can be hard to digest. With a style of bland writing and commonsensical advice, these books typically read like college texts and taste like rubber.

A medley of comedy, guidance, and case examples, *How to Lose a Custody Battle* will not leave a bad taste in your mouth! From the title alone, this book offers much more flavor than what you may expect from a typical self-help guide.

Dr. Saturley approaches the self-help genre with a playful banter that is both refreshing and cleverly insightful. *How To Lose a Custody Battle* is a satirical salute to bad parenting decisions.

While presenting how to make bad situations worse, Dr. Saturley instills wise counsel through "Doc Joe's Words of Wisdom" without the residual feeling of being lectured. The words between the lines speak on how a parent should behave. If there's anyone who knows how to be a good parent, it would be Dr. Saturley.

I have enjoyed working on this book with my father. Discussing his ideas and watching them come to life has been a delightful experience. I hope you will enjoy reading (as I have) a satirical approach to self-help.

~ Justin J. Saturley

How To Lose A Custody Battle

1
IF YOU WANT TO LOSE CUSTODY...
SHOW UP LATE FOR COURT

One way to ensure that you lose custody of your children is to send a message to the judge that you are an irresponsible parent. Show up late. While you can never be exactly sure what message you are sending to a judge, you can be reassured that this strategy doesn't grant you any brownie points.

There are essentially three types of individuals who are consistently late for appointments:

1. Scatterbrains - Scattered and unorganized people don't plan well and often show up late for appointments. They are late for work and never pay their bills on time. You can readily anticipate that utilities get shut off at least once or twice a year because they forgot to pay their bill. These people often suffer from attention deficit disorder.

2. White Rabbits - Remember the White Rabbit from *Alice in Wonderland*? "I'm late, I'm late, for a very important date!" Overly scheduled people make too many appointments, overbook themselves, and often show up late for appointments. These are people who schedule two meetings at the same time, or schedule meetings so close together that they don't allow for traffic or travel time. These people think they are impervious to the influence of time.

3. The Fashionably Late - Narcissistic people are often late for appointments. These individuals send the message that their time is more important than yours, and since they are more important, you should have to wait for them. Judges don't like that.

It doesn't matter in which category you fit. It also won't matter what excuse you have for being late. Showing up late for a court hearing is a loud and clear message. Have no fear, your judge will understand just what type of individual you are. Any excuse for lateness will show that you aren't the best parent to have the children the majority of the time.

Doc Joe's Words of Wisdom

When an appointment has been set, the conscientious parent will:

1. show up on time, or
2. show up early.

Whether you are flying-by-the-edge-of-your-seat as a parent or not, timeliness goes a long way to say that you are at least trying to do your best.

Don't ever show up late for court, and don't let your attorney show up late either. Never make a judge wait for your case; it sets a precedent and makes the judge question your level of responsibility. Judges rarely observe families in the hallway. But, they are informed by their assistants and bailiffs about what goes on. Judges have many eyes and ears throughout the courthouse, as well as in the community. While it is improper for them to take anything under consideration that isn't directly presented as evidence during a hearing or trial, they are still human. Everyone is influenced by the things we see, do, or think we know. Your judge is no different, and if they think you are uncaring and arrogant because you are late for a hearing, you will pay the price of their perception of you.

Arthur and Amy

Arthur and Amy were married for twelve years. They were good parents, and they had two wonderful children. Both Amy and Arthur were educated and loved their children very much. Arthur was very disciplined and had spent many years in the military. He ran things in a militaristic way. Amy finally grew tired of Arthur's conservative and inflexible ways and sought a divorce.

Arthur was a successful business man and had many employees. He was phenomenally smart. He managed his business from his house or from the road and much of the time via his cell phone. He scheduled conference calls and took them while he was with his kids. He scheduled calls in between business presentations and while traveling for both business and pleasure.

The problem for Arthur was, despite his years of military training and knowing how essential timeliness is, he had come to believe that his time was more important than anyone else's. He began leaving his house late and showing up late for most of his important meetings. His tardiness even interfered in meetings with his very expensive attorney. Of course his attorney didn't mind (Arthur was being charged at the rate of $350.00 per hour).

There were significant reasons why the children should not have been placed with Amy. We will never know how the judge might have ruled if Arthur hadn't shown up a half hour late on the first day of his trial. We also won't know how the judge might have ruled if Arthur had shown up on time for the second and third day of his trial.

When Arthur showed up late on the fourth day of his divorce trial, the judge was more than frustrated. He summarily chastised him for his repeated tardiness and threatened to toss him in jail if he was late again by so much as ten seconds.

The children now spend the vast majority of their time with Amy and see Arthur on alternating weekends and one night per week for dinner.

Arthur occasionally shows up on time.

2
IF YOU WANT TO LOSE CUSTODY...
LET YOUR RACIST FLAG FLY

If you are a bigot, you've already won half the battle. Undoubtedly you've already done some things to alienate your neighbors, coworkers, or other people in your community, and they will be ready to testify against you.   Good going.   The court won't want your children to spend the majority of time with you, because you will be instilling fear in them toward anyone who is different.

Keep doing what you're doing.   If you haven't already attended some distinctly discriminatory function like a Ku Klux Klan meeting, then get on the internet as fast as you can to find your local chapter. Make sure that you get some sort of regalia when you attend the first meeting. Make yourself known. At the first meeting, try to shake everyone's hand, get to know as many people as possible and announce your name to them. Let your new acquaintances know you have children and be especially sure your new brethren know you are involved in a custody battle.   Inquire if anyone will come to testify that you are a member in good standing with their organization. Make sure you join and pay your dues.   For an added touch, let your membership card fall out of your pocket when the court ordered social worker stops by to make a surprise home visit.

If you happen to be lucky enough to have been assigned a judge of a different race or culture, make sure you do some negative blogging on the internet and sign your name to it. That way, if someone happens to google your name, they'll be sure to find it and know just how prejudiced (I mean loyal) you are.

If you have a female judge and you are a father, make sure you talk condescendingly to them.   Quote some scripture that alludes to women submitting to men. It's also a nice touch if you can slip something negative about your mother into the conversation.

If you have a male judge and you are a mother, spout off about how all men are pigs. Let an idle "under your breath" comment slip that the judge keeps looking at you in nasty and vulgar ways. Come off as a femi-nazi.

Doc Joe's Words of Wisdom

The average person has some prejudices against someone. We would like to think that we are unbiased and don't discriminate against anyone, but the reality is that almost everyone discriminates. Some individuals don't like left handed folks or those who are overweight. Others may not like lazy or ignorant people. The bottom line is, if you are a good parent, you will do everything you can to combat your biases and keep from passing them on to your children.

If you are a racist, get some help. If you have had some bad experiences and were raised by parents who didn't teach you that everyone is created equal, then let me be the first to tell you that all people are the same. It doesn't matter where they come from, what they eat, or what their culture or skin color is. If we begin to treat others like we want to be treated, the world will soon be a better place.

If you have some biases (and you don't want them to effect you or the outcome of your case), it might be wise for you to learn how to keep your mouth shut. Don't go around "waving your flag" that people with darker skin or eyes not shaped like yours are inferior. You are illustrating to the world that you are the inferior one.

It would be wise for you to sign up for some sensitivity training and learn about other cultures. Avoid any friends you have who talk in bigoted ways and make sure that you build relationships with people who are different from you.

Bart and Betty

Bart and Betty were a partying couple. He was a local celebrity, and she was a trophy wife. They enjoyed their wild nights together, but their drunken and drugged out conditions often led to domestic incidents with police responses. Both had been married previously and had children who were being raised by their former spouses.

Bart was the product of uneducated, foreign-born parents. Betty was the product of a broken home and years of abuse at the hands of her mother and her multiple boyfriends. Bart and Betty enrolled in rehab upon the discovery that Betty was pregnant. Both achieved short term sobriety. But as any addict will tell you, initial sobriety is easy. Finding a quality sobriety that lasts is the difficult part.

Bart was often interviewed by the media. Betty was happy staying at home raising their newborn. For addicts, relapse is always knocking at the door. Both of them relapsed on their child's second birthday celebration. Within three weeks of their relapse, the police responded to their home five times. The first time that Bart slapped Betty in a drunken rage, she packed her bags and moved into her mother's home with their daughter.

Betty was as much of a mess as Bart. She continued to drink and went out partying as much as he did. But celebrity Bart continued to be interviewed by the media. He spewed hate. He hated black people. He hated Arabs. He hated Jewish people, and most of all, he hated women. He provided multiple sound bites that aired during sweeps weeks for hyped ratings. Bart was a gold mine for the media.

Betty's condition worsened, and she was so deep in her addiction and alcoholism that some days she couldn't get out of bed until late afternoon. It was a Godsend that her mother was there to take care of the child. Neither Betty nor Bart were great parents.

Bart's judge was a white man who had been raised in the deep south. He was also around for the tumultuous 50's and 60's. He even watched Martin Luther King, Jr., deliver a civil rights speech.

It was Bart's prejudices that sank his case, not his parenting abilities (or disabilities).

Bart learned it's a small world after all.

3
IF YOU WANT TO LOSE CUSTODY...
EXPOSE YOUR CHILDREN TO YOUR NEW PARAMOUR

If the separation of parents hasn't had the negative impact on your children that you intended it to have, the act of initiating a brand new relationship with someone else will.

Attract attention to yourself by quickly getting involved in a new relationship. If you plan to use this strategy, the quicker you get seriously involved with a new lover, the better.

Find someone who is particularly offensive. This will emphasize the lack of empathy you have for your children.

Consider the following people as good candidates: your children's current or former teacher, a stripper, their soccer coach, or an immediate or remote relative (remote relatives are less effective). Your wife's sister is always a nice choice.

Whatever you do, DON'T warn your children about the new relationship. Let them find out on their own. Create as much shock value as possible. Top this strategy off by having your paramour move into your home as soon as possible. Surprise the children on their return from parenting time with the other parent.

If your new significant other has their own children, convert your child's room into a new room for your lover's child. Move your child's possessions into the garage. Let your child sleep on the couch. This is an assured way to offend your child and turn them against you. The confusion, anger, and betrayal that will result will surely work against your chances to secure custody.

Doc Joe's Words of Wisdom
Good parents don't expose their children to new paramours until they are sure the new person is a relatively permanent fixture in their lives. Doing anything else will just confuse the children.

Children are impressionable at any age. After divorce, children are particularly vulnerable and susceptible to confusion at the hands of their parents. Children grow up with the impression their parents will love each other and stay married forever.

Adult children of divorce report the one thing they wish they could change is that their parents would get back together. There is just something unsettling when parents separate.

After a divorce, wait before you introduce your kids to your new paramour. The typical rule of thumb is not to introduce children to your dating partner for at least six months from your first date.

If you intend to marry someone new, consider letting time pass after you introduce your children. Allow adequate courtship and adjustment time between your new love interest and your children.

Carrie and Carl
Carrie and Carl divorced in May. They had a quick divorce, and it took only three months from the filing until it was completed. They didn't have many assets to argue over, and they wanted to split the children's time equally between themselves. They got along after the divorce and rarely disagreed.

Carl became concerned after his children came home from their first week with their mother. They had met "Mommy's new friend." He was already spending overnights at her house.

Carl tried to talk to Carrie about his concerns. But, Carrie's new relationship had clouded her judgment. She was so enamored with her new boyfriend that she wouldn't even discuss the matter.

The children's grades began to drop, and their son began to say inappropriate things to girls during recess.

Carl filed a motion for a rehearing of the final issues of the case. The judge decided that Carrie was not such a good influence on her children. The children now only see their mother every other weekend.

Carrie learned it was important to protect her children from exposure (to her new paramour).

4
IF YOU WANT TO LOSE CUSTODY...
DRESS TO IMPRESS

Throw fashion and social appropriateness out the window. Put on a tie dyed tee and ragged blue jeans. Let your hair grow long and be unkempt (grow out your beard if you are a man). Wear love beads. Flash the peace sign at everyone. This behavior still has the same impact it did in the late sixties and early seventies.

Show up disheveled and dirty. It can really boost your image if you have significant body odor. This can be an excellent strategy particularly if the other parent is clean and well kept. The contrast will speak volumes to the judge.

Make sure your shirt is not buttoned appropriately. In other words, leave the top open. It can't look accidental. Your look needs to be deliberate. A silk shirt (or fake silk) that shows your skin underneath is also effective.

Cut-offs in the courtroom are always a nice touch. Judges really scratch their heads when litigants show up in the courtroom dressed in this manner. Your inappropriate dress will flabbergast the judge. If you choose the shorts route, make sure to accompany them with ratty flip flops and a wrinkled t-shirt.

Spend some money on clothing for court. Buy a new suit. Make sure it is flashy and over the top. If you are a woman, make sure your clothes are two sizes too small and accentuate all the right areas. Communicate that you are available to anyone with a large enough bank account. If you are a man, make sure your suit communicates you are looking to become a pimp or gigolo. Reflective material is always handsome and makes an announcement about you before you enter the room.

Dressing in work clothes is a good idea, too. Showing up in them sends the message that you didn't have time to go home and change, and you're on your way back to work after the hearing. It sends the message that you are a working stiff and didn't know any better. It also speaks to your ignorance of social norms.

Doc Joe's Words of Wisdom

"Dress to impress" has long been a standard. It's reasonable to assume if you want to be taken seriously as a parent, you will show up to court looking conservative and like a mainstream individual.

People with common sense know how to dress appropriately for any special occasion. Good parents know it is important to make a good impression at a court hearing. Men should be dressed in a coat and tie. Women should wear a dress, skirt, or slacks and a nice blouse. If you don't own "nicer" clothes, borrow them from a family member or neighbor so that you can make the right impression.

Grow up and dress your age and look like a mature responsible parent. If you dress to make your male judge drool, you'll discover that it does nothing but hurt your case. A man who looks like he just stepped off the macho boat will equally hurt his case, too.

If you don't know how to look, go to a trusted family friend or a professional and ask their advice. Better yet, ask your attorney how you should dress.

Darlene and Dave

Darlene and Dave were happily married for several years and brought some lovely children into this world. Dave had inherited much wealth from his family, and his perspective about how you should look in social situations was skewed. Both Dave and Darlene were very social drinkers to the point that they overindulged. After a girl's night out, Darlene got a DUI coming home and decided it was time to sober up.

The longer Darlene was sober the more conflict entered their marriage. At some point it spelled the end.

Darlene was a sober drunk. She no longer drank, but her personality was caustic. She yelled at the children and treated them poorly. The children enjoyed Dave, and he had a significant relationship with all three of them.

Dave's social standing in society often caused people not to tell him the truth. If he asked if he looked good, the common reply was that he did. He needed praise, and it was obvious.

He was advised to show up for his trial in a suit. He opted to show up in loafers with no socks, a silk shirt and a tennis sweater neatly over his shoulders. His appearance took the judge by surprise, and he was quickly deemed an out of touch socialite. Darlene got the children with very little consideration of Dave as a primary parent.

Dave still doesn't get it. He can't even buy a clue.

5
IF YOU WANT TO LOSE CUSTODY...
TAKE A CALL DURING COURT

All motion stops when a phone rings at an inappropriate moment. People lose their train of thought, stop talking, and everyone stares at the offender in amazement. This is a sure fire method of getting the judge to realize you have questionable judgment. There is nothing more attention grabbing than when a cell phone rings during court.

Timing is important. Arrange to have someone call you in the middle of the hearing. The best way to take advantage of this strategy is to answer the phone rather than silence it. Look at the judge when your phone rings, and then look at your phone. Put your finger up and announce that you have to take the call. It won't matter whether you take the call in the courtroom or get up and leave.

After you have taken the call, spend plenty of time talking to the person even if you have to fake it. Five or ten minutes on the phone will be sufficient. You may not get the chance to drag it out before the judge holds you in contempt. If this occurs, you will know you have succeeded.

Doc Joe's Words of Wisdom
A good parent knows when it is and is not appropriate to use their cell phone. Proper cell phone etiquette requires the silencing of phones in certain settings.

If you are a socially responsible and appropriate adult, you will know when it is okay to use your phone. It isn't okay to use your cell phone when you are having dinner in a fine restaurant or during a movie. It isn't okay for your phone to ring during church, a wedding, or during class. Make a regular habit of putting your cell phone on mute, silence, or vibrate mode.

Everyone can make a mistake. People who create disturbances with their cell phones are searching and screaming for attention. Learn to get attention in more productive and less intrusive ways.

ALWAYS silence your cell phone before entering court or the judge's chambers. It is preferable to turn your phone off, because even the buzzing of a cell phone is distracting, and the judge will not take it kindly.

Evelyn and Earl

Evelyn and Earl were not a couple made in heaven. Earl was considerably older than Evelyn, and he was used to having things his way. He was a hard worker and earned a good living. Earl courted Evelyn for several months before asking her mother for her hand in marriage. Evelyn's father left the family early in Evelyn's life because he was abusive.

Earl's age was closer to Evelyn's mother than to Evelyn. He was charming and appropriate. Evelyn's mother liked Earl more than Evelyn did. Earl was her mother's favorite son-in-law.

Earl was running several different businesses at the same time. He had a knack for keeping financial matters in his head, and his employees enjoyed working for him despite his controlling nature. He was a fair employer.

Earl was always available to his managers whenever they needed him. He had a group of convenience stores that were open twenty-four hours a day. He had three different cell phones that he carried constantly.

Earl's beliefs about running his businesses caused problems for him and Evelyn. They couldn't go on vacation, because he had to be available. Even when they would go out to dinner with friends, they were often disturbed by business calls. Earl refused to be without his cell phones.

When Evelyn finally grew tired of Earl's love for business rather than for her and the children, she decided to divorce him. Earl loved his children, and they enjoyed their time with their father. Unfortunately, his time with the children was always interrupted by phone calls.

Earl's phone rang during the first court hearing. It surprised and frustrated the judge. It rang during the second hearing and infuriated the judge. Earl's phones did not ring during the third hearing. But, all three of them were the on the table in the hearing room. All three vibrated at the same time. The judge enthusiastically ruled that Earl would have to leave his phones in his car for any future hearings.

Evelyn thought Earl deserved plenty of time with the children despite her frustration with the phone situation. The judge disagreed. The judge's frustration level was so high, that he ruled that Earl was to have minimal time with the children. The judge also recommended that Earl take some business management classes.

Earl quickly learned for whom the bell tolls (or the phone rings).

6
IF YOU WANT TO LOSE CUSTODY...
BE YOUR OWN ATTORNEY

One of the great things about the legal system in the United States is that you can act as your own attorney. You need no training. The term for this is *Pro Se*. Pretend you know what you are doing and march into court with a briefcase and legal pad. Act as your own attorney.

Don't do any research before going to court and certainly don't ask for any assistance. Pretend you know how to object and file motions. Judges often feel empathy for Pro Se litigants and allow them significant leeway in the court room. You can counteract the judge's empathy for you by being disrespectful and reminding the judge that you don't want or need any special treatment.

Make sure that you miss filing dates and don't follow procedure. Call the judge's assistant and annoy them with stupid questions like how to spell the judge's name and what your case number is.

When you finally get a hearing date, mumble when you ask questions. Be condescending or accusatory. It is helpful if you interrupt the judge, and then ask multiple questions about issues that have already been addressed.

When you file motions, sign them in crayon and fill them with irrelevant information. Make sure you have plenty of grammatical errors and misspelled words. Confuse everyone by using illogical arguments.

Send the message that you are haughty and arrogant and feel that you are smarter than anyone else in the courtroom. After all, this is your day in court.

Doc Joe's Words of Wisdom
Good parents hire competent attorneys to represent them in court. They realize law is a specialty that a layperson is not

prepared to practice. Attempting to practice family law against an experienced attorney is not a good idea.

Don't act as your own attorney in family court. If you really want what is best for your children, find the money and hire a good attorney. There are so many nuances about the family law system that even good attorneys have to often check their law books for specific procedures.

Occasionally, a smart parent acts as their own attorney and is successful. This is possible, but not recommended. The average person does not possess the verbal or research skills required to mount an effective strategy for a courtroom battle.

Finding a good attorney can be a challenge. Good attorneys are not cheap and finding a bargain can mean that you don't have what you need. You get what you pay for. Be careful. Do your research and find an attorney who is reasonably priced, smart, and can proceed to court to fight your battle. Be cautious of attorneys who always settle their cases. While this is typically a good thing to do in family law cases, if you hire an attorney who is afraid to litigate, you may be settling for less than your children deserve.

Frank and Fanny
Frank and Fanny were an odd couple. Frank was a conservative business man and Fanny was a free spirited young woman. They produced one child before their ill fated marriage ended. At the divorce they decided they should equally share time of their child, Tammy.

Fanny soon took up residence with a man closer to her age, and Frank soon remarried a woman who had a child of her own. Frank and his new wife soon had another child. When Tammy turned nine her school work went downhill. Frank had ignored his fears about Fanny's influence on Tammy. Fanny's boyfriend made a good living, but he was odd, and there were questions about his legitimacy as a business man.

Frank decided to seek more time for himself with Tammy and less time with her mother. The court ordered an evaluation of the entire family. The report was issued and was highly critical of Fanny and her boyfriend. Frank was no angel, and the report was equally, if not more, condemning of him.

Fanny hired attorney at the beginning of the case who was paid for by her boyfriend. As time passed, he became bored, and as more information was uncovered about him, he became frustrated with the whole affair and withdrew his financial support.

Fanny began to represent herself. While she was fine at filing motions and responses, when it came time for the trial, she was overwhelmed. She didn't know how to object or what to object to. She didn't understand about hearsay testimony and couldn't phrase questions properly. She was unsuccessful at getting negative information about Frank submitted into evidence.

While she had the right idea, her inability to properly represent herself doomed her case. Fanny now sees her daughter on alternating weekends.

Caveat emptor (buyer beware)! Fanny got her money's worth.

7
IF YOU WANT TO LOSE CUSTODY...
NEVER COMMUNICATE WITH THE OTHER PARENT

Give the other parent the silent treatment. By refusing to communicate in any fashion with the other parent, you will create some sort of difficulty for your children. Be a child. Plug your ears and say, "I can't hear you!"

You don't need a good reason for not communicating, simply don't do it. If you want to voice a reason for not communicating, say you feel manipulated, or the other parent is condescending or insulting to you. Be less than convincing.

Cut off all communication. The sillier and less logical you make your argument the better. Remember that your objective is to leave people scratching their heads and looking at you like you came from another planet. They have to think you are borderline crazy.

Beware of emails in high conflict cases. An email has an indirect lure that may elicit a response from you. This is not in your best interest if you want to lose the custody battle. Emails are a ploy used by parenting coordinators and judges. They realize that high conflict parents know how to push each other's buttons.

If you are ordered to communicate, use the circumstances to your advantage. Making yourself look bad can be easy. Wait until the last minute to send emails to make arrangements for the children. Send them late and claim they must have been lost in cyberspace. As an alternative, refuse to communicate via email even after you have been ordered by the judge to do so. See the alternate strategy, **Treat An Order Like A Suggestion**.

Communicate in nasty and vulgar ways such as accusing the other parent of tawdry or illegal activity. Call them unacceptable names and YELL at them in the email by USING ALL CAPS. Raise the level of conflict high enough in emails so that your judge will limit your communication.

Doc Joe's Words of Wisdom

Communication between parents is the most successful way to co-parent children during and after divorce. When two parents communicate, children avoid emotional conflicts, because when parents are communicating, things get worked out.

Good parents communicate no matter how difficult or unpleasant it becomes. They do not make unilateral decisions. Good parents find a medium through which to communicate that is effective and efficient (it may be in person, over the phone, or through text or email messages).

In high conflict divorces, parents communicate best by email. There are some reasons for this:

1. **Big Brother is watching**. Because emails are monitored, people tend not to send offensive communications.

2. **The infamous paper trail**. When you use email, there is always a paper trail. This tends to make parents more cautious about what they say in writing to the other parent, because they know it could be used against them.

3. **Time to think before we speak**. People can become emotionally charged in face to face exchanges. The outrageous things we are apt to say to someone's face tend to be subdued in emails.

Learn how to communicate appropriately with the other parent. Learn to communicate without making accusations or provoking the other parent. Don't use vulgarities.

Your child will benefit if you and the other parent can learn to get along. If you can't get along, learn how to communicate succinctly through emails. Do your best to reduce (rather than elevate) the conflict.

If the court orders you to communicate in a specific way, at a certain time of day, or through a specific medium, then follow the order exactly the way it is written. Do not go outside the order.

Gwendolyn and George
Gwendolyn and George never communicated well even when they were married. After the divorce, George refused to have any contact with Gwendolyn. He reported to anyone who would listen that he had nothing to say to her, and he certainly had no interest in anything she had to say.

George was obsessive. He enjoyed provoking verbal altercations. He also tended toward paranoia. George took every word literally, and it was virtually impossible to have a normal conversation with him. Everyone felt like they constantly walked on eggshells when dealing with George. As for Gwendolyn, she came with her own set of oddities, but they were minor compared to George's.

The judge was particularly patient during their divorce and subsequent court hearings. But, he soon grew tired when they returned month after month on George's minor fault finding expeditions. George's attorney, despite making a handsome income from the many motions he filed, also grew weary. It was clear to the judge that the parents were unable to communicate, and he wrote an order limiting their contact.

The judge ordered George and Gwendolyn to exchange one email per day, which was limited to discussions involving the children. Each email was to be limited to 100 words.

George consistently violated the order. He was always quick to jump on Gwendolyn. He would berate her and often sent emails in ALL CAPS, with occasional profanity. Rarely did he ever send one that had less than 150 words.

Gwendolyn's frustration became so high that she took copies of the emails to her attorney and asked what could be done. Her attorney filed a motion for contempt and subsequently asked that George be evaluated because of the content of the emails.

The judge was concerned about the content of George's emails and his blatant disregard for the court's order. He ordered that George's time with his children be temporarily suspended and that a psychological evaluation should take place.

As a result, George's only contact with his teenage boys is under supervised conditions.

And, he still hasn't learned EMAIL ETIQUETTE.

8
IF YOU WANT TO LOSE CUSTODY...
BROADCAST YOURSELF

This strategy is highly charged because we live in a relatively conservative and sexually stringent country. In some European countries prostitutes are available in store front windows, and sex is a casual practice. This is not the case in the United States. Despite nudist resorts and legalized prostitution in one state, judges still take a conservative view of the sexual exploits of parents in their courts.

It's easy and fairly inexpensive to join an internet adult site that will give you access to other kinky adults. Many sites let you post pictures of yourself and allow you to post your wildest fantasies. So *go* for it!

Broadcast and market yourself. The difficulty with this strategy, as with some of the others, is being discovered. Hand out pamphlets to coworkers that say "Check out my website." Send a broadcast email to as many people as you know. Watch out for spam filters. You may need to disguise your email with a catchy subject line ("This is Important") and send it to your spouse's best friends asking them to join.

Doc Joe's Words of Wisdom
Good parents keep their physical and sexual relationships behind closed doors. They do not advertise on the internet that they participate in deviant activities.

If you are a parent of underage children, keep your physical relationship limited to significant others. If you have trouble meeting people with whom you have things in common, limit your online escapades to legitimate and mainstream social sites.

Engaging in sexual liaisons with strangers (or strange people) will bring problems to your life. Many people think they can hide their fetishes and other unusual lifestyles from others. Escaping to foreign countries to indulge your fantasies will not work. Your exploits will catch up with you sooner or later.

Wait until your children are grown. At least then they can deal with your alternative lifestyle with adult brains.

Harry and Henrietta

Harry and Henrietta were married for ten years. Both were broken individuals and they were never able to love the other. They did, however, produce three lovely children.

Harry and Henrietta posted profiles on an adult hookup website. Both also knew of the other parent's posting, so it was done with full knowledge and implied permission. Problems escalated when Henrietta decided that she had more feelings for someone she met on the internet, than she did for Harry. Eventually, Henrietta filed for divorce.

Accusations flew from one side of the courtroom to the other. The case was full of sexual content. The media became interested, and their case became a three ring circus. Harry accused Henrietta of being an adulteress and a sexual addict. Henrietta accused Harry of being a deviate. The judge declared both of them morally bankrupt and said neither deserved the children.

The case continues in family court unresolved. The children bounce back and forth between households.

The parents continue their wild lifestyles. The children were exposed to inappropriate situations. Two of the children went to their school guidance counselor. Social services was called the children are now in foster care.

Two wrongs don't make it right.

9

IF YOU WANT TO LOSE CUSTODY...
MISS A COURT DATE

Missing a court hearing is an excellent way to illustrate what kind of parent you are to the judge. Initially, it will be presumed that something bad has happened to you. Make sure that you aren't doing anything important on the day that you are supposed to be in court. Take the day off from work and go fishing or some other recreational pursuit that will infuriate the judge.

When you miss a court date the other side often wins by default. Sometimes you get an understanding judge and instead of proceeding without you, they will postpone the hearing until it can be rescheduled. It will be unfortunate if you have such a judge. This strategy is only successful when the judge makes a ruling in your absence. Missing a rescheduled hearing certainly increases your chance of a default decision.

The judge will typically instruct your attorney to attempt to reach you. Don't answer your phone when he calls, fishing is more important than your kids.

To have more impact you can put a message on your cell phone indicating that you are out pampering yourself with some activity, took the day off from work to watch a golf tournament, went bowling, etc. Remember, you want to impress the judge with your lack of responsibility and send the message that you are invested in wasting his or her time.

Beware of judges with no sense of humor when using this strategy. The humorless have been known to issue bench warrants for arrest for not showing up for hearings.

Doc Joe's Words of Wisdom
Good parents make appointments and show up for them on time. In family law cases either the attorneys or the judge sets the appointment times (also known as court dates). A normal individual knows that it is very important to show up for these court hearings.

Make court dates your top priority. Don't show up late and for goodness sake, don't miss them, no matter what. Judges are people, and their job is to judge you based on a variety of factors including whether you have made your time in front of them a priority. If you treat a judge (and their time) with disrespect, they will take that under consideration, and it will come back to bite you.

Irene and Irving

Irene and Irving were a wealthy couple. Irving had inherited a trust fund from his grandfather and had gone to college and landed a high paying position in the financial world. Irene came from a wealthy family and had been showered with the finer things during her childhood. They were a handsome couple, and their three children were healthy, smart and talented. When the financial markets turned sour, Irving's personal investments suffered considerable losses. The financial strain on the family brought such significant stress to the marriage that it didn't survive. Irene filed for divorce at the suggestion of her dad, and she moved into her parent's home with the children.

Irving didn't exist very well on his own because he had been taken care of for most of his life. His mother had babied him and often served him breakfast in bed while he was in high school. Irving was not required to do chores as a child, and he didn't suffer normal consequences in college for his partying. His father sat on the board of directors of the college and professors passed him. Irene hadn't asked much of him during the marriage because his income allowed them housekeepers and a nanny for the children.

Irene got Irving out of bed on time and on the way to work so he wouldn't be late. Irving's secretary was the one who reminded him of appointments, anniversaries and birthdays. But when Irving's employer began to downsize, and his secretary had to be shared with three other financial managers, the secretary's attention to Irving's calendar became a thing of the past.

Without the assistance he was used to, Irving's life became a tangled mess. He began to miss appointments and was late to pick up the children on his weekends.

The first time that Irving didn't show up for a court hearing, the judge instructed Irving's attorney to go out in the hall to call and find out where he was. Irving's lawyer returned to announce that it was an oversight on Irving's part, and he was attending a high level conference across town. There was inadequate time for Irving to get to the courthouse to conduct the hearing. The judge was understanding.

When Irving hadn't arrived on time for the next hearing the judge again instructed Irving's attorney to go out in the hall and attempt to locate his client. When the attorney returned to announce that Irving was out of town on business, the judge's blood boiled. She ruled him in contempt and conducted the hearing in Irving's absence. Testimony was presented about how many times Irving had been late picking up the children, and on two occasions completely forgot about them at after school functions. The judge ruled that Irving should be evaluated and ordered supervised visitation until the completion of the evaluation. Irving missed the first appointment for the evaluation.

Irving sees his children one weekend per month. The paternal grandmother is responsible for picking up the children and returning them on his weekends.

Time waits for no man. Irving learned he was just a man.

10
IF YOU WANT TO LOSE CUSTODY...
ALIENATE YOUR CHILDREN

Tell the children how awful the other parent is. When you want to lose a custody battle there is no better strategy than parental alienation. Remind the kids of every fault the other parent has exhibited. Make up stuff that isn't true.

Stomp out every positive emotion they have for the other parent. If the children tell you anything positive, make sure you tell them they are wrong.

Discourage your children from going to the other parent's home. Convince them they are unwanted by the other parent. When the other parent calls to talk to the children, hang up on them. Never tell them the other parent called.

"Forget" to inform the other parent of an important school event or recital. Then tell the children the other parent didn't come because they aren't loved.

Tell them the other parent is crazy. Make up lies. Children are so impressionable that you will implant false memories in them. Soon they will begin to make up their own stories about the other parent.

Doc Joe's Words of Wisdom
Parental Alienation takes place in every divorce. It happens even when you try to avoid it. Children overhear you talking negatively about the other parent. They see the frustration written on your face. Avoid alienating your child at all costs.

Remind your child that they are loved by both you and the other parent. Do this even when you are angry and would prefer to unload about the other parent. Parental alienation will come back to haunt you in the future. A day will come when your children will realize that you lied, and they will hold it against you.

Children can find enough to be angry about without you assisting them. Keep your garbage out of their heads.

Many experts have thrown out terms like "Malicious Mother Syndrome" and "Parental Alienation Syndrome" in attempts to bring a classification system and common language to this phenomenon. Hot debate continues on the topic of parental alienation.

Don't participate in this type of activity. It will harm your children permanently.

Jack and Jill
Jack and Jill went up the hill to fetch a pail of water. Sorry, that was a different Jack and Jill.

Jack and Jill were childhood sweethearts. They married young, worked hard, and started a family. They were happy with each other in the early years of their marriage.

Times change, and so did the relationship between Jack and Jill. Jack started his own business at Jill's urging. He also began a series of extramarital affairs and ultimately took on a mistress when his income increased. Jill continued to raise the children and did her best to ignore Jack's affairs.

After many years of marriage the couple separated. Jack told the children it was Jill who wanted the divorce. He pleaded ignorance and filled the children's heads with fantastical lies that painted their mother in a bad light. Jack continued the brainwashing after the separation.

Jill began to have more and more difficulty with the children. They were rebelling and by the end of the first year of their parent's separation, the children stopped spending time with their mother. Jack wouldn't send them because he claimed they were afraid. He found a mental health professional who supported his stance on not sending the children.

The case dragged on. The children were successfully alienated against Jill. Her attorney suggested it would be better if she just wrote off the children until they became adults.

Jack and Jill's daughter got pregnant before she was sixteen. One of their sons dropped out of high school and entered rehab. One son disappeared and hasn't been seen in over a year.

Jack and Jill went up the hill, but it was the children who came tumbling back down.

11
IF YOU WANT TO LOSE CUSTODY...
LET YOUR CHILD BE THE PARENT

Act irresponsibly and naive by letting your child post whatever they want on their MySpace or Facebook pages.

Tell your child they can decide with whom they are going to live. It doesn't matter what your state statutes are, tell your child they have the right to make this decision.

Allow your child to make decisions about their health. Don't make them get their immunizations or brush their teeth no matter how horrific their breath becomes (or how rotten their teeth get). Let them drink beer.

Let your children go out for the evening without knowing what they are doing. Believe them when they tell you they are going to the movies. Don't bother with details about who is driving them. Checking up on the children or being concerned about their safety is what "uncool" parents do.

Believe whatever your child tells you. When your child comes home reeking of smoke with bloodshot eyes, accept it when they tell you they went to a sad movie, and they don't know why they smell odd. When you find a pack of cigarettes in their backpack, pretend to believe someone must have put it there by mistake.

Be sure to communicate to the other parent that you are letting the child make the decisions, and you will support whatever the child wants to do no matter what. Emphasize your belief that your child is old enough to make up their mind about any important matters in their life (even if they're not).

Doc Joe's Words of Wisdom
Good parents listen to their children but make the important decisions for them. We cannot expect children to make difficult and mature decisions that adults are supposed to make for them. A good parent makes the tough decisions about what their children should or should not be doing.

Learn to have some discernment and wisdom. Learn not to be gullible. Just because something is written in a book does not mean it is true. Learn to question normal convention and think for yourself. Trust what your gut instincts tell you and begin to realize that people (including your children) tell lies to avoid unpleasant circumstances.

Good parents do not believe everything their children tell them, nor do they believe everything they are told by the other parent. The average person doesn't believe everything they are told, no matter who told them or where they heard it. Wise people check out information and decide on their own what to believe or whose advice to follow. You should be wary of what your children give you for excuses. If you are a good parent, you will occasionally check up on them to make sure they are being accountable and telling you the truth.

Learn to be the adult for your children. The decisions about whether to watch Bugs Bunny or Sponge Bob can be left up to your children. Decisions about doing homework, if they will have breakfast, or if they will go and spend time with the other parent should **not** be left up to children.

It will always be easier for you not to make decisions. Some parents (subconsciously) avoid making decisions so that they will never be wrong or never be blamed for what went wrong in their children's lives. It is your responsibility to act as an adult and make the tough decisions. See to it that your children spend time with the other parent even when they don't want to.

Karen and Kenny

Karen and Kenny were a loving couple until Karen's grandmother died and left her a sizable inheritance. Kenny was lazy. The couple soon found their differences led to separation. Both were close to the children, Karl and Kim, so they decided it best to enter into a fifty percent time sharing arrangement.

Karen generously gave Kenny a chunk of her inheritance. He indulged the children in everything they wanted. She continued to be conservative. Kenny bought Karl a motor bike and let him ride on the streets even though he had no license. Karl dumped his bike at the beginning of the week when he was at his father's house. Kenny didn't take his son to the doctor because he didn't want to go. By the time he returned to his mother's, Karl's road rash was terribly infected.

Their daughter, Kim, began having parties at Kenny's house during her father's weeks of parenting. Kenny bought beer for the parties, though none of the kids were old enough to drink. Kim, a freshman in high school, started dating a boy who was eighteen.

As time passed the children wanted to spend more time at dad's and less at mom's. They began to be unruly for their mother and would call Kenny complaining they had been grounded. Karen was constantly hearing from the children, "Dad lets us do that!"

When Kim came to Karen's for her week with two huge hickeys, Karen decided enough was enough and filed a motion for the judge to intervene. After all, Kim was only fourteen.

Testimony illustrated that neither child had a consistent bedtime or any regular routine at Kenny's. The children were often tardy for school (if they went at all) when they stayed at Kenny's. The pictures of Kim's neck made the judge's decision easy.

Kenny's lack of parenting drew attention to his household. He now sees his children every other weekend. Social Services has been out to visit and has an open investigation.

No one ever said parenting was easy.

12
IF YOU WANT TO LOSE CUSTODY...
GET ARRESTED

No matter what you have done to get arrested, it will bring special attention to you and to your custody case. Before engaging in this strategy there are two old phrases to remember:

1. "Don't do the crime if you can't do the time."
2. "People don't plan to fail. They fail to plan."

Arrests for violence, drug smuggling or sex crimes are the most likely to assist you in your endeavor to lose a custody battle. An arrest for a bar brawl may or may not make it into the papers. If the judge or someone else related to your case is thorough, they will probably check your name against the police blotter before your next court hearing.

Up the stakes under this strategy and resist arrest and wrestle with a police officer. Choosing this route will result in an arrest for battery on a police officer. That will raise some eyebrows. After your arrest, make sure to mention you have an upcoming court hearing in your custody case. This will get the gossip mill grinding, and your judge's bailiff will get wind of your arrest.

Drug arrests are always an interesting twist in a custody battle. It is important to plan before pursuing this category of arrest. Getting arrested for a small amount of marijuana may or may not work against you. Some judges view any illegal activity as an ultimate sin. Others view things like minor violations to be no big deal.

Don't get arrested on a Friday. You won't be arraigned until Monday, and your weekend will be ruined. If you are looking for a weekend to sober up, then this strategy has multiple benefits.

Doc Joe's Words of Wisdom
Good parenting and getting arrested do not go hand in hand.

I am still amazed by people. I have never been arrested. My wife hasn't been arrested, nor have either of my children. Most of my friends have never been arrested. None of my professional colleagues have been arrested (that I know of). So, I am truly amazed when I come across people in evaluations that have been arrested multiple times and think it is no big deal.

Some people say that the only people who don't get arrested are smart people. I don't know if that is true. If you want to be considered a good parent, you will keep your nose clean and stay out of trouble.

Lee and Leslie
Leslie married Lee out of sheer spite to enrage her father. Lee proved his father-in-law wrong and became a hard worker. He started his own business and was grossing over a million dollars by the third year of their marriage.

Lee and Leslie had two children. When the family wasn't on vacation, Lee spent most of his time at the business. Lee spent time with the children, but tended to ignore his wife. Leslie was emotionally unfulfilled, and after months of begging Lee to attend couple's counseling, she found an attorney.

The custody papers were being prepared for signatures when Leslie found out about Lee's arrest. She read about it on the back page of the newspaper. It was a small article about men soliciting prostitutes. Lee's name was among ten other men who had offered an undercover officer money for sex.

Leslie called Lee immediately. He refused to discuss the matter. Leslie didn't have any other details, and the newspaper article was sketchy. She told her attorney to delay the signing of the custody papers.

Two weeks later Leslie read about her husband again. Lee was arrested for drunken driving and possession of drug paraphernalia. The article stated that Lee had a questionable woman with him at the time of his arrest. When Leslie did research on the woman's name, she discovered multiple arrests for prostitution.

Leslie no longer trusted Lee. Despite Lee's insistence that he was innocent, she was unwilling to accept his statements. She instructed her attorney to begin a custody battle. Lee's legal problems were still simmering when the trial began.

Lee's testimony at the first custody hearing sank him as he provided vague answers to questions. Lee's time with his children was reduced to afternoon visits only. He is not allowed to transport his children, and he has no overnight parenting time.

Lee didn't lose the custody battle because he was a bad father. He lost it because of his bad behaviors.

13
IF YOU WANT TO LOSE CUSTODY...
TREAT AN ORDER LIKE A SUGGESTION

Treating an order as if it were only a suggestion illustrates to the judge that you are a poor choice as a parent. You can clearly communicate just how irresponsible you are by thumbing your nose at the judge's authority.

Justify in your mind that judges don't really mean, "You can't do this!" or "You can't do that!"

When a judge orders you NOT to have any contact with the other parent, ignore that order and call them. Stop by their place of work and start up a conversation. Show the judge that you know better than they do. After all, you are the master of your own destiny. Who cares if the District Attorney's Office decides to prosecute you for violation of a restraining order? That will show the judge who the real boss is.

Convince yourself that they can't tell you what you can or can't do. Who do they think they are? You are not in the military. No one should be able "order" you around.

When the judge orders you to return your children to the other parent on Sunday night at 6:00 PM, don't return them until after 8:00 PM. Better yet, keep them until Monday morning.

When a judge orders that your children can only participate in one extra curricular activity per semester, sign them up for two. This will again show the judge who the real boss is. Never consult the other parent.

<u>Doc Joe's Words of Wisdom</u>
In family law, the decisions of the judge are referred to as orders. Orders in family court are designed to be viewed just like orders in the military. They are things to be followed without question and without exception.

Good parents follow the law. They don't skirt the law, and they don't interpret the law to fit their needs. A court order is just like the law. It is the law when it comes to your family court case.

If you don't want to be held in contempt, it is wise to follow every order the judge signs. Don't over interpret or under interpret them. Orders signed by judges are typically clear, and there is no need for interpretation. They are typically written in plain language. If they aren't, ask your attorney to file a motion for an explanation of exactly what the judge wants.

Court orders are not court suggestions! If you treat the judge's orders like they are suggestions you can anticipate running into trouble somewhere down the line. In some states, when you treat an order like a suggestion you cannot only be held in contempt, but the judge has the option to throw you in jail for your disrespect.

Mary and Michael
Mary and Michael had four well behaved children. The children became closer to their mother as the marriage began to fail.

After the separation, conflict between Michael and his children escalated when his paramour was around. The children did not like their father's girlfriend. They felt their father was being disrespectful to their mother by having a girlfriend.

Mary asked the judge to limit the paramour's contact with the children. The judge agreed that the girlfriend's presence was not helping the children adjust to the divorce. He ordered until the divorce was final, the paramour was not to be present for parenting time.

Michael was a masculine and macho male. He wasn't about to let some outsider tell him what he could and couldn't do. When he wanted to spend time with his girlfriend, he skipped parenting time.

The divorce was complicated and dragged on for months. Little progress was made, and there was no significant communication between Michael and Mary.

Michael had the children for a thirty day uninterrupted stretch during the summer months. He rented a condo in the islands and wanted to take the children. Mike also wanted to have his girlfriend there. He decided to ignore the judge's order, and they all went to the islands for two weeks.

Upon Mike's return to the states, he was met with a scheduled court hearing for contempt. The hearing determined that Mike was in direct violation of the judge's order. He was found in contempt, fined, had to pay court fees, and his summer vacation time with the children was reduced to one week per month.

Mike discovered the hard way that orders are *not* suggestions.

14
IF YOU WANT TO LOSE CUSTODY...
MAKE AN AGREEMENT AND BREAK IT

When you have entered into a temporary (or permanent) agreement with the other parent, break it. If you make an agreement not to move outside a certain school zone or particular radius, move just far enough outside the zone to cause problems. If you have agreed not to move out of the county, do so anyway.

Agree to postpone introducing your children to a new paramour until you have dated them for six months. Then, arrange for an introductory dinner within the first couple of weeks. Agree to alternate years in which you claim the children as tax deductions and then, be the first to file each year and claim them. You'll save hundreds on your taxes.

Agree to let the other parent choose the child's sporting activities in the spring and then sign them up for baseball in December. Or, agree that your son can play football in the fall, then withdraw your consent saying it is too rough on the first day of practice.

Agree to allow the other parent to take the children on an expensive cruise, then decide a week before they set sail that you won't give up the passports. Better yet, file an emergency injunction with the court claiming the other parent won't return them to the United States. Claim this is an attempt by the other parent to kidnap your children to a foreign nation.

Doc Joe's Words of Wisdom
When a person makes a written agreement, we expect them to abide by that agreement. We also expect people to live by their verbal agreements. When a good parent makes an agreement, we expect them to keep their promise.

Before you sign your marital settlement agreement, get some good advice. Take it home, read it and sleep on it. Take it to a family member or wise friend and have them read it. Let them help you sort through all the things that might be problematic in the future. No one can predict all the changes that will take place in your life. Ask someone to play "Devil's Advocate" and poke holes in the fine points of the document.

Don't take the advice of an attorney who doesn't specialize in family law. Get good advice and be prepared to go back to the negotiation table. Once you sign the divorce papers, they are more difficult to change.

If you make an agreement, or if the judge makes a final order, live by it. Don't find grey areas in the document and don't make assumptions. If it reads that you have to obtain permission from the other parent to do something, get their permission before you do it. Otherwise, you may find yourself on the "outside looking in."

Nancy and Norm

Nancy and Norm's divorce settlement was very specific (for the children's sake neither parent was able to move outside of the county unless they agreed to it in writing).

Nancy married shortly after the divorce. She and her new husband bought a house two miles over the county line (they got a great bargain). Nancy never bothered to get a written agreement from Norm. She relied on the advice of the real estate attorney who explained that family law judges give parents a "five mile grace zone."

Nancy's geographical relocation wasn't problematic until the children entered formal school. Norm wanted the children to attend a school near his home. Nancy wanted the children to attend a school near her. When they couldn't agree on a school, they ended up back in court.

Some judges like 50/50 parenting time. But, Norm and Nancy's judge felt it is important for a child to wake up in the same bed in the same home every morning before school. He believed it was important for a child's stability and school performance.

The judge couldn't believe Nancy's violation of the agreement. He found it particularly disturbing that Nancy was in law enforcement. The judge inquired, "If someone is only slightly over the legal limit for drunkenness, do we give them grace and allow them to go on their merry way?" Nancy could only hang her head in shame.

It was an easy case for the judge to decide. Nancy was clearly in violation of the marital settlement agreement. Her argument that she had been misled by the real estate attorney held no water for the judge. He ruled the children would attend school near Norm's home. They wake up on all school mornings at his home.

Nancy, who now lives by her agreements, has the children every other weekend and sees them Wednesday nights for a short dinner.

When it comes to family law matters, Nancy no longer takes advice from real estate attorneys.

15
IF YOU WANT TO LOSE CUSTODY...
LET A CRIMINAL WATCH YOUR CHILDREN

Taking a criminal into your home is great way to make your judge and other people wonder what is wrong with you. A criminal with a violent history, drug charges or someone with convictions of violence against children will really put you under the judge's microscope.

Draw attention to your actions. You can harbor all the fugitives you want, but unless the judge or the other parent finds out about your scheme, it is useless. Play loud music late into the night and disturb your neighbors. Annoying your neighbors adequately results in calls to the police.

Start a rumor that you are providing housing to criminals. It will only be a rumor until it is confirmed by your former spouse.

Leave your children with this individual as a care taker. When your children go home to the other parent and relate some horrific story, you'll get a panicked call from the other parent. Tell them who you rent a room to is none of their business.

Doc Joe's Words of Wisdom
The average person does not take in borders who have criminal pasts. The average parent does not let people stay in their homes if they have criminal histories. This is true even if they are former friends or relatives. They might allow a relative or old high school or college friend to spend one night on the couch or a weekend in the guest bedroom. They certainly don't allow extended stays.

If you can't figure out how ridiculous it is to accept someone in your home with a criminal past, you may not be a good candidate to be exposed to your children anyway. It doesn't matter how much your friend claims to be innocent, don't let them stay with you. Don't be manipulated by your brother (the bum) who has been in and out of jail since childhood. Don't believe anyone's sob story that they have nowhere to live. If you want to keep your children you'll grow a backbone and learn to say "NO" to these less than desirables.

Owen and Olivia

Owen and Olivia were never married. They lived together and had a plump little baby boy they named Otto. Owen was sort of a celebrity in town and made a lot of money. Many people kept telling Owen that Olivia was just a gold digger but he didn't want to believe them. Then one day he came home and found most of his possessions missing and Olivia and Otto gone. He scratched his head and decided maybe his friends were right after all.

Owen was a kind hearted guy. But he was arrogant and thought he knew more than most of the people who advised him. He was loyal to his friends to a fault. He paid Olivia lots of money initially and she let him have Otto over half the time.

When Owen and Olivia went to mediation, it was discovered that Owen had a childhood friend, Fast Johnny, living with him at his home. Olivia said she didn't want Otto visiting at Owen's house because Fast Johnny had a criminal conviction. Owen became outraged. He told his attorney that Fast Johnny was a good friend and a loyal brother. He argued that Olivia had no right to suggest Fast Johnny shouldn't be around Otto. Owen threw a fit and said the issue was non-negotiable and that Fast Johnny was staying with him no matter what.

Owen was asked what Fast Johnny's conviction were for. He didn't know. Owen was ignorant and put his foot down on this issue. He needed to know the facts about Fast Johnny.

Owen made two quick phone calls. Fast Johnny's conviction was for assault and battery. But, Owen believed Johnny when he said he was framed. It didn't matter to the judge.

Owen lost the battle. He sees Otto every other weekend.

Ignorance and arrogance can be expensive.

16
IF YOU WANT TO LOSE CUSTODY...
DRUNK DIAL THE PEOPLE
INVOLVED IN YOUR CASE

The key to leaving drunken messages for people is to make it blatantly known how intoxicated you are. A slight slurring of the words won't be terribly effective. Too many people will give you the benefit of the doubt.

Do your research before you make the drunken calls. Find the best numbers to leave messages for the professionals involved in your case. Make sure you leave a message at your spouse's attorney's office.

Use of this strategy requires creativity. Speak directly to the answering machine or voicemail.

Leave a particularly long message. Mumble on as long as possible until you are cut off or until you fall asleep. While you are sober you may want to write a script. You won't believe how difficult it is to leave long messages.

Doc Joe's Words of Wisdom
It is always considered bad form to leave drunken messages for anyone. Many people have done it at one time or another. My guess is that almost everyone has made the mistake of leaving a slightly intoxicated message for someone. It might have been a parent when we were in college, a roommate, or even one of our significant others. Even if you never left one for somebody else, the chances are great that you have received one.

If you have a problem with drugs or alcohol, please get help. It is disturbing to receive phone calls from a slurring drunk.

Intoxicated and lonely people talk about the injustices of their lives. They feel abandoned or wronged. They are in need of friendship, companionship, or therapy.

If this is you, go find a good therapist. At a minimum, practice self restraint and avoid making these calls. The best rule is not to make any phone calls when you are intoxicated.

Penny and Paul

Penny and Paul were married for many years. Paul's career required him to travel most of the time, and he was gone for two or three weeks at a time. He would be home for two or three days before he was off again.

Penny also worked and raised the children. The children were angry and depressed. Penny was also depressed. Their social stature made it unacceptable to discuss or display their feelings.

Penny was more than a social drinker. The longer she was married, the more she drank. She was more fun when drunk, but her intoxicated condition was distressing to the children.

The economy turned sour, and Paul began working from a home office. He was home most of the time. He created an alliance with the children. Penny's drinking did not decrease.

Paul could no longer tolerate Penny's drinking. He offered her one chance to enter rehab, but she refused. He moved out the following morning.

The attorneys agreed a custody evaluation would be best to settle the dispute. A psychologist determined the children should temporarily reside with the father.

Penny raised the children from birth. But, her drunkenness caused them to resent her. She began to drink even more. Before long, her loneliness became overwhelming, and she began to make phone calls. At first, she called her family. Soon, she began calling random numbers on her cell phone just to hear people's voices.

Penny's friends were getting intoxicated calls in the early morning hours. When they quit answering their phones, Penny's calling radius began to widen. She left long drunken messages at her attorney's office. He was her friend and couldn't bring himself to tell her to stop. Her calls continued to escalate. Penny was soon leaving five minute messages on her custody evaluator's voicemail. The messages were slurred and illogical ramblings.

The custody evaluator suggested that Paul w as the best parent. He also recommended that Penny enter alcohol rehabilitation. Penny still hasn't sobered up. The judge agreed on both points.

Penny's children were initially forced to have supervised parenting time with their mother. Penny was unhappy with the arrangements and discontinued them. Her oldest child cut off all contact when he turned 18. Her youngest child continues to live with Peter and has no contact with her.

Penny continues to leave long drunken messages on the evaluator's voicemail.

Loose lips sink ships.

17
IF YOU WANT TO LOSE CUSTODY...
HIRE AN INCOMPETENT ATTORNEY

If you don't want to be blamed for losing custody of your children, hire an incompetent attorney. How can anyone blame *you* when your incompetent attorney loses the custody battle? Everyone can point at your attorney and say how bad they were and what they should have done, but didn't. You will get their sympathy vote. Hire an attorney that you know isn't up the the task (one who is slow witted, misses deadlines and isn't prepared for court).

Hire an attorney who specializes in something other than family law. Hiring a criminal attorney for a family law case is a good idea. After all, if Johnnie Cochran can get O.J. off, then a good criminal attorney ought to be able to get you your kids.

Better yet, hire a real estate attorney to fight your custody battle. Hire a good litigator (a good trial attorney). This will look like a winning combination. Litigators think the final trial is where all the decisions are made. This is not the case in family law. Family law is a true speciality and if you hire an attorney who only dabbles in family law, you will probably lose.

Hire a friend who is an attorney. A bro will always have your back. Right? This will remove all objectivity, and you won't get honest feedback about your case. Hiring a friend who is an attorney in your family law case is a winning proposition for losing.

Doc Joe's Words of Wisdom
Fifty percent of all attorneys graduate in the bottom half of their class. Think about that!

Nobody would want a surgeon cutting them open who graduated in the bottom half of their class. The same holds true if you want to win a custody battle.

Good parents do their research before hiring an attorney. They find out about their records and how they operate in the courtroom. Good parents hire an attorney with a good reputation, one they can afford, and one who can assist them in reaching the goal of what is best for their children.

Do your research **before** you hire an attorney. Don't just ask friends. Call the Bar, call some local evaluators and ask for referrals. Interview the attorney before you hire them. Research your attorney's record. Find out if they have been disciplined. Do an internet search and a search of your local paper to see if any news articles have been written about them.

Don't just hire an attorney you've seen on a billboard. Hire an attorney that graduated in the top half of their class, not the bottom half. Do some detective work.

Find out if your attorney settles the majority of their cases (or if they tend to litigate the majority of their cases). This alone does not mean much, but you don't want to spend thousands of dollars to go to trial on a simple divorce case that should be settled between the attorneys. You also don't want to settle a case because you have an inexperienced attorney who is afraid to litigate.

Hiring a friend who is an attorney to fight your case is rarely a good idea. They act as your friend first and your attorney second. They don't have any objectivity about your case, and they aren't able to give you the best advice. When they see you doing things wrong, they are less apt to tell you. The biggest trouble is that when they try to give you good advice, you won't hear their advice in the manner you need to. Don't hire a friend as your attorney.

<u>Queeny and Quentin</u>
Queeny and Quentin married as teens. Quentin was mean at heart and loved his money. Neither of them was very bright, but Queeny had good instincts. She was the one who suggested that Quentin open a business. He followed her advice and was soon making good money.

Over the years, they had three children who were spoiled rotten brats. They wanted for nothing and were disagreeable. Quentin was verbally abusive to all of them, and Queeny's frustration often boiled over to the children. It was a conflictual home. There was never any peace. Interestingly, they all seemed to have great love for each other. Some families learn about love despite the high conflict or sometimes because of it.

It was never quite clear what led to the divorce. It may have been Quentin's womanizing, or it may have been that Queeny found someone who really cared about her.

The divorce was ugly. Quentin hired a good attorney, and Queeny was thrown out of the house on a bogus domestic violence charge. Quentin controlled all the money, and Queeny settled for an incompetent attorney (whom I will refer to as Daffy) who could barely tie his shoes. Daffy came from a long line of attorneys. His mother was an attorney, and his maternal grandparents were judges. But, Daffy was lazy and spoiled. Daffy reminded Queeny of her children, and she was unable to fire him because she felt sorry for him.

Even a half decent attorney could have gotten temporary financial support for Queeny. A good attorney could have convinced the court that Quentin should be paying for her legal fees. But, her disheveled attorney spent most of his time drawing pictures on his legal pad. His questioning of the witnesses was painfully inadequate.

Quentin was in contempt of court on so many issues that it overwhelmed Daffy. He couldn't comprehend how to file the appropriate motions.

The judge ordered the children to attend counseling with Queeny. Quentin refused to bring them and refused to pay. Rather than file a motion for contempt with the court, Daffy filed a motion to have Queeny evaluated (an attempt to show there was nothing wrong with her).

It was worst circus the judge had ever seen. Unfortunately, judges cannot intervene and tell a parent how woefully inadequate their attorney is performing.

Queeny got the worst fleecing the judge had ever seen in his years on the family bench. Quentin had successfully hidden tens of thousands of dollars. The children were successfully alienated from their mother. And, Quentin got the family home.

Queeny hasn't seen her children since 2002.

You get what you pay for.

18
IF YOU WANT TO LOSE CUSTODY...
IGNORE YOUR MENTAL ILLNESS

If you suffer from some type of mental illness, whether it is properly diagnosed or not, the best strategy to lose a custody battle is to ignore the problem. If your disorder is readily apparent to most lay people and you have something like bipolar disorder or schizophrenia, then it will be much easier to lose a battle.

When you feel an episode coming on, just ignore it and let it run its course. This strategy shouldn't require much effort on your part. If you are bipolar and starting a manic phase, let it take off in full flight. Beware though, as this will undoubtedly have side effects, wild financial purchases, cursing at the moon while staying up all night, or getting arrested for some other wildly exotic behavior.

If you aren't crazy, it's never too late to start practicing.

If you can't pull off a serious condition like bipolar disorder or schizophrenia, you can always come up with something less drastic but almost as effective. A good depressive episode where you stay on your couch for several days eating everything in sight and not bathing tends to catch people's attention. If someone calls, sound particularly pathetic and self destructive when you answer. It is important to draw attention to yourself while you are hidden away behind the closed shades (or else no one will notice and the strategy will be ineffective).

General panic attacks and anxiety disorders are also effective. These conditions tend to totally isolate individuals from society and make them completely ineffective as parents. You can even develop a case of agoraphobia.

Do not seek out professional help. Self medicate if you think it is helpful to your cause. Remember, do whatever it takes to send the message that you are an unacceptable choice as a parent.

Doc Joe's Words of Wisdom

Being a good parent means knowing when you need help, especially when you have mental illness. Being mentally ill does not preclude someone from being a good parent.

As society has progressed into the twenty-first century, people have become more sensitized to mental health issues, and the family courts are more knowledgeable than ever.

Mental illness, by itself, does not make a bad parent. Just like a physical illness, mental illness can typically be controlled and treated in a fashion that makes it a non-issue for parenting.

Mental illness comes in many forms, has varying symptoms and differing severities. At one end of the mental illness spectrum we have depression and anxiety disorders. In the midrange we find disorders like obsessive-compulsiveness and eating disorders. At the other end of the spectrum we have bipolar and personality disorders. Many good parents have these types of disorders.

With the exception of a few of the more severe pathologies, mental illness can be treated and controlled to allow for good parenting.

If you suffer from some type of psychological condition, go find competent help. As in any professional field there are good practitioners and not so good. Finding good assistance can be quite a challenge. Do your research, ask someone you trust for a good referral.

I can promise you one thing, if you ignore your illness, it will undoubtedly get worse and your children will suffer.

Robin and Raul

Robin and Raul were known from the start as the crazy couple, "Rabid Raul and Racey Robin." They earned their nicknames before they married, and everyone warned them they should not have children. Raul and Robin proved people wrong, kept their mental illness in check, and were successfully married for three years before Robin became pregnant.

Robin and Raul were diagnosed as bipolar and were faithful about their monthly appointments with their psychiatrist. They were good to their children.

When Raul's mother died, he went into a tail spin and started into a manic swing. He avoided his typical routine and skipped his psychiatric appointment for the first time in six years. He started staying up late, drinking and missing work. He began yelling at Robin and the kids. His family tried to intervene. His doctor left multiple messages for Raul. None of them were returned.

Robin tolerated his condition for two months. She knew it was Raul's responsibility to take care of himself, but he refused to get help. The first time Raul didn't come home after a night of drinking, she had the locks changed and sent the children to stay at her mother's.

When Raul came home the next day, he broke every window in the house. Having not slept, Raul became paranoid, believing his neighbors were out to get him. The neighbors were frightened by all the breaking glass and called the police. Raul was involuntarily hospitalized.

Raul spent two weeks in the hospital. Robin's faith in him was shattered, and she filed for divorce. Her application for a domestic violence injunction was granted because of Raul's erratic behavior at the house.

Raul has been stable since his release, but the damage was already done. He sees his children every other weekend and one afternoon each week. An ounce of prevention would have alleviated the need for a pound of cure.

In this case, ignorance was not bliss.

19
IF YOU WANT TO LOSE CUSTODY...
VIOLATE A COURT ORDER

If there is a particular order from the court forbidding you to enter the other parent's residence, do it anyway.

Many times there are clauses in court orders that people don't read. For instance, if you have been ordered to participate with a Parenting Coordinator, you may discover a clause in the order that reads, "Entry of Residence: Neither party will enter the residence of the other except as pursuant to the written agreement of the parties, or by order of the court." I can't tell you how many couples I worked with over the years that neglected to read the order, and as a result, didn't know they were ordered to stay out of the other person's residence.

Most children have keys to their parent's homes. While your child is with you, or after your child has gone to bed, sneak over to the other parent's home and use your child's key to see what you can find. Make sure one of the neighbors sees you and calls the police. If you are really bold, make sure you are in the house when the other parent comes home.

If you don't mind spending a couple of days, weeks or months in jail, you can always do some vandalism to their home. Spray paint graffiti on the walls. Smear food and other things on the living room walls. Judges take notice when a parent has been arrested for such things.

Installing secret cameras or other types of recording technology is a really nice touch if you can afford it. This can result in one or more incarcerations depending on what type of surveillance equipment you install. It might only be a misdemeanor offense, but if you get really technical and creative, you might be able to rack up two or three felonies along the way. If you time it properly, you can be brought to family court in your jail clothes.

Doc Joe's Words of Wisdom
The average person in our society obeys the law. They do not break and enter, steal, shoplift, or commit other crimes like

robbery or assault.   Good parents are the same as average people, they obey the majority of the laws of the land.

After you get divorced get a new life. You got divorced for a reason, and whether you wanted to get divorced or not, it is a signal to you to start over.   Quit focusing on what the other parent is up to.   It is hard enough for most of us to create one satisfactory life (our own) and detaching or disengaging from your former spouse is what you are supposed to do.

If you are obsessively focused on your former mate, get some help. Short term medication may be required. One thing is for sure, if you continue to focus on your former spouse, you will begin to make mistakes, get yourself in trouble, and both you and your children will suffer the consequences.

Scott and Samantha

Scott and Samantha's marriage was troubled from the beginning. Both had grown up in families of divorce. Neither had known a healthy family.   They tried to make a normal family after the children were born, but the odds were stacked against them.   They couldn't agree on any issues about the marriage or about raising the children.

They limped through fifteen years of marriage.   After the divorce they were so used to each other, and knew so little about being alone they had trouble separating.   Scott was always wondering what Samantha was doing. He didn't stalk her, but he constantly questioned the children about their mother's activities.

The conflict between them continued after the divorce.   There was so much conflict the judge ordered a parenting coordinator be assigned to their case. The judge's order was clear that both parties were forbidden from entering the other's residence without written permission.

They agreed that when Samantha went out of town for a business trip that the children would stay with Scott. The oldest child would be brought to Samantha's apartment each afternoon to feed the cat and change the litter.   Scott couldn't resist the temptation and went into Samantha's apartment and began looking around. He went through all of her things, and the child reported it to her mother.

Scott was charged with violation of the court's order. Samantha got temporary decision making power about the children.

Scott's inability to resist the temptation cost him dearly. The judge determined that because Scott had violated the court's order about non-entry, that he did not have good enough sense to be making important decisions about the children.

Samantha now makes all important decisions about the children, including educational, medical and extracurricular activities.

Rules are *not* made to be broken.

20
IF YOU WANT TO LOSE CUSTODY...
USE EXTREME DISCIPLINE METHODS

Use of extreme discipline methods is a sure fire way to lose a custody battle. These techniques include:

- soap in the mouth
- whipping posts
- hot sauce
- electric cattle prods
- stun guns

You can be assured of a visit from a child and family services investigator if you start washing out your child's mouth with soap. So, go for it! Make sure your child's teacher, bus driver or sports coach knows. If you don't think your child will tell anyone, you can proudly announce what you have done to one of the above individuals.

You can always justify any method of discipline by exclaiming, "It was done to me and look how I turned out!"

If your child uses profanity, wash out their mouth with hot sauce. It really won't hurt them significantly, but it will make other adults wonder about you.

Remember to take care of your personal affairs before using this type of strategy. It is probable that you may spend a few hours being interviewed and investigated for your disciplinary methods. You also run the chance of incarceration so make sure you have someone to take care of your goldfish while you are behind bars.

Doc Joe's Words of Wisdom
It never happened to me. I was a good kid. But I can tell you that as I grew up a number of my friends had their mouths washed out with soap. That was a different time in a different type of society. It was before we had any significant social service agencies to protect children.

Good parents take care of their children in loving and caring ways. If they become frustrated, as all parents do, they find productive ways to funnel that frustration and do not take it out on their children. Good parents DO NOT use their children as targets.

NEVER ABUSE YOUR CHILDREN. If you aren't smart enough to realize how bad the aforementioned discipline techniques are, then turn your children over to your spouse and resign from being a parent.

Tom and Tammy
Tom and Tammy were both successful in their careers and looked like upper middle class America. Tom rescued Tammy from her abusive home when they met at the community college. They looked like the perfect couple. They were both attractive, athletic and appeared on the surface to be quite taken with each other. Behind the doors of their apartment the fights were vicious and often violent. Things were thrown by Tom but rarely aimed at Tammy. Tammy would scratch and kick in retaliation for Tom's tantrums. Holes were punched in the walls, and the deposits on their first three apartments were forfeited.

The fighting continued even after the birth of the children. The children learned to throw tantrums and manipulate their mother. Tom worked long hours and rarely participated in parenting.

One day, Tammy went shopping and left Tom alone at home to watch the boys. He became so frustrated and angry at their misbehavior that he chose a line of extreme discipline. He marched them into the kitchen and took habanero peppers out of the refrigerator. He forced each boy to eat one.

The boys cried and began to vomit. This infuriated Tom. He reached for the bottle of hot sauce. The boys ran from the house screaming in fear. The next door neighbor heard the commotion and met the boys outside. She called social services about Tom.

Tom and Tammy are now divorced. Tammy has taken some parenting courses. She has better control over the boys. Their behavior has improved.

Tom took an anger management course and a domestic violence awareness course. They didn't do him any good. Tom continues to have limited and supervised contact with the boys.

Tom has never won any parenting awards (but he did win an award for his hot sauce).

21
IF YOU WANT TO LOSE CUSTODY...
POST THINGS ON THE INTERNET

It is quite effective when you post racy things on the internet. Many couples have taken intimate photos of their sexual encounters, and some even have videos of their exploits.

Upload your videos to a website. The only problem you face in this strategy, is that sometimes it is difficult to trace the postings back to your account.

Start your own website by buying a domain name and posting the other parent's pictures or videos there. Make sure the domain you buy can be traced back to you easily. A domain name like, www.JohnsExWifesPics.com can be a real eye catcher.

If you don't have any racy or raunchy pictures or videos, use photoshop to cut and paste the other parent's face onto an extra juicy piece of pornography. Don't make it look too good, remember the point is to get caught. Make sure that it doesn't look professional and don't try to make money off the pictures. You don't want to make it appear that you are a legitimate business person.

Create your own blog about how bad a person the other parent is. Exaggerate in every respect and don't say anything good about them. It is very important that you paint the ugliest and most outlandish picture of this person possible.

If you want to lose the battle by looking like a pervert, post naked pictures of yourself on the internet.

Post things on the internet about your judge. They don't have to be the truth and the juicier the better. You could look up some controversial case that was located in your county and then write outlandish things about your judge. It won't matter whether your judge was really involved in that case or not. Remember, people believe what they read no matter where they find it. When your judge finds out what you put on the internet, it will be the end of your chances to be the primary parent.

Doc Joe's Words of Wisdom

There are acceptable and unacceptable things to post on the internet. Personal information is often found in many of the popular social networking sites. Personal information is also found on some of the less popular and exotic networking sites. It is considered unacceptable to put information on any site that concerns anyone other than yourself. Posting information about anyone else on the internet is a violation of their rights. Good parents don't post information about the other parent without their permission. Good parents don't post personal information about their children on the internet. Good single parents refrain from posting pictures and information about their children on dating websites.

Stay away from the internet. It is a tempting world in which to seek revenge. Most people think you can post things anonymously. Guess what? You can't. Even the best of hackers get caught sooner rather than later. Unless you are a top notch hacker, you won't have any luck posting anonymously.

Be an honorable person and dispose of whatever incriminating things you may have on your former spouse. Burn them or return them. Despite what you may think about revenge, it always comes back to bite you harder in the end.

Ursula and Ulysses

Ursula and Ulysses were an interesting couple. Ulysses was a good looking and well built man. Ursula was an attractive woman and men often stared. Unfortunately, they were also into the swinging lifestyle. As with many couples who engage in that kind of lifestyle, they soon found that the intimacy they once thought they shared with each other was dashed by their lack of fidelity.

Ulysses was an insecure and somewhat paranoid man. When Ursula filed for divorce, he became convinced it was over another man with whom they had swung. It was not, but

Ulysses wasn't as interested in the truth as he was in revenge and hurting Ursula. Ulysses had pictures and videos of Ursula and decided to post them on the internet. He concluded this would bring negative attention, and the judge would be forced to give the children to him.

Ulysses built a website and began selling Ursula's exploits. When Ursula found out about the site she was aghast, and her attorney filed an Emergency Motion for Ulysses to stop. The court hearing was a circus, and the judge was displeased with both parents over their lifestyles. But, he concluded that neither parent had exposed their children to their lifestyles. Therefore, what the parents did behind closed doors was none of the court's business.

The judge was disturbed by Ulysses' behavior. Ursula had discovered the website when the father of one of her children's friends mentioned it to her at a PTA meeting. He asked her what kind of money she was making. Ursula was taken by complete surprise and highly embarrassed.

The judge ruled that Ulysses had gone out of bounds. He concluded Ulysses had placed his children in psychological risk because of what he had tried to do to their mother.

Ulysses was ordered to shut down the site and turn over all lewd materials to Ursula. Ulysses now pays a substantial amount of alimony to Ursula and sees the children every other weekend.

What goes around, comes around.

22
IF YOU WANT TO LOSE CUSTODY...
CLAIM YOU CAN'T PAY CHILD SUPPORT
(THEN TAKE AN EXPENSIVE VACATION)

This strategy comes from the old school (in other words, it's been around forever). While this may be an old strategy, it is still an effective one. Don't pay your child support, no matter what. This will always get the attention from the court it deserves.

By strategically not paying child support, you loudly broadcast that you no longer care about how the children are living and are not interested in their well being. This is the message you want conveyed to the judge.

As the holidays approach, you can demonstrate just what a slimy no good parent you are by claiming that the economy has turned, and you are up to your neck in debt. Fall behind in your child support so the other parent has to scrimp and can't buy the usual allotment of holiday gifts.

Make this look really good. Claim that your new girlfriend's children have emergency medical needs, or your car needed some expensive repair, or your parent's life time home is in foreclosure. The important thing is to come up with some really good cover story so the other parent will have plenty of sympathy for you.

Be really convincing. The other parent will help break the news to the children and will be willing to forgo or at least postpone your child support payments.

As soon as the pressure is off, announce to the children that you are going on a wildly expensive and exotic vacation. Going all out is a nice touch. Ski in Aspen, jungle trek in Costa Rica or SCUBA dive in Australia. They are all effective shockers.

Doc Joe's Words of Wisdom
The idea or philosophy behind child support is that it allows the parent who is receiving the support to maintain a lifestyle for

the children that is equivalent to the lifestyle the family was accustomed to before the divorce. Child support is meant to be spent on the children and their activities and needs.

Good parents ordered to pay child support do just that, they pay their child support on time and in good faith. If they fall on hard financial times, a good parent calls the other parent and asks for a little extra time to pay. Or, they seek some other alternative means to satisfy the situation until the money is available. The average individual doesn't just ignore their financial responsibilities or allow their monthly debt to accumulate to significantly unacceptable levels.

Valerie and Vern
Valerie and Vern were married under ideal circumstances. Both were college athletes and top graduates in their college classes. They went to law school together and graduated at the top of their class. They were recruited by top firms in the same city and paid top dollar for their sixty hour work weeks.

They decided to start a family. Being attorneys, they negotiated their agreement because they knew that Valerie was about to take a significant break from her career, and her earning potential would take a blow.

When Valerie asked Vern to cut back on his hours at the firm to spend time with her and the children, he refused. Vern was even insulted that she would ask.

Their quarreling was intense because both were trained litigators. When discussion of divorce arose, the intensity became catastrophic.

Valerie returned to the practice of law, and the children went into daycare. They temporarily agreed to an equal time share arrangement with the children.

Valerie's divorce attorney convinced the judge that Valerie was due compensation far above the norm. Vern was dismayed that he had to pay her such a substantial amount each month. But, he knew it was only temporary.

Vern began dating immediately and lavishly entertained his dates. He was living beyond his means and soon maxing out his credit cards.

At first, Vern was just a few days late with his child support and alimony. Then, he skipped a payment. Valerie was concerned and called him. He claimed the firm was not doing as well as the previous year, and his quarterly bonuses were insufficient. Valerie accepted Vern's explanations and agreed to allow him time to make up his support payments.

Valerie exploded in rage when she learned that Vern had spent two weeks in Jamaica at a very expensive resort. She had her attorney file contempt charges for being late with payments. She also filed for a time sharing arrangement in which she would be the primary care taker.

By the hearing date, Vern was so burdened with debt that he was two more months behind in child support, and Valerie had pictures of his lavish Jamaican vacation.

The hearing was expectedly ugly for Vern. The judge was irate over Vern's financial conduct, and the pictures of his Jamaican vacation played heavily. Vern was not only required to catch up on his child support, he was fined by the court, and held in contempt. Vern had to pay for Valerie's legal fees, and Valerie has the children eighty percent of the time.

Don't do the crime, if you can't do the time (or pay the child support).

23
IF YOU WANT TO LOSE CUSTODY...
TREAT YOUR CHILDREN DIFFERENTLY

Treat your children differently. This is especially important if you have one child who is talented or one has special needs. When one child is good in sports and the other is not, make sure to pay special attention to the one to the neglect of the other.

Miss important dates and appointments for one of your children. Make sure you take the gifted child to practice or games when the non-gifted child has scheduled appointments. Don't ever think about making alternate arrangements.

If you have two children who are gifted, alternate your attention from month to month. Give extra attention to the oldest child on odd months. Reverse this strategy for the younger child. The alternative to this is to choose one child to neglect on a consistent basis. Make sure you choose to ignore the child who is less gifted.

If you have a challenged child or one with special needs, this strategy is extremely effective.

Doc Joe's Words of Wisdom
"Good" parents treat their children equally no matter how "special" they are.

The idea behind good or appropriate parenting is to treat each child the same. Favoring one child over another or disfavoring a child, no matter what the reasons, will ultimately lead to difficulties. This is common knowledge and even discussed in the Bible in the story of Joseph and the multi-colored coat. The father paid special attention to Joseph causing extreme jealousy in his older brothers. They ultimately beat Joseph and left him for dead.

Children need to be loved equally no matter how talented they are or are not. How we treat our children is how we communicate our love to them. You can tell your child that you love them all day long, but if you treat them differently, or you treat your only child poorly, they will get the real message.

All children are unique. Even identical twins have different abilities. It is important to identify each child's unique qualities and gifts. Help the child build upon those gifts. Some children are gifted in math while others are gifted at sports. Some children have musical gifts while others are skilled dancers. Every one of us has a gift. As a parent, it is our job to nurture the talents of our children.

The time, energy and resources that you devote to your children's gifts need to be fair and equal. Find a way to exert the same amount of energy and resources to each child. Some children's talents require an investment of time while others require an investment of money. Each child should feel they are being given equal resources.

Walter and Wendy
Walter and Wendy's children were as different as night and day. Winston, the older of the two boys, was a gifted hockey star, while Wally enjoyed acting and dancing. Walter had been an athlete as a younger man. He, therefore, focused his attention almost exclusively on Winston. He took Winston to games, practiced with him in the driveway until after dark and always bought him new skates and souvenirs from each professional hockey game they attended.

Walter never took Wally to his dance practices. He never attended any of Wally's recitals. Walter was always busy at work or at Winston's games when Wally's recitals were scheduled. Wally told his mother he didn't mind that his father was never in attendance.

Winston would bully, push and punch his brother. Walter always told Wendy that it was "normal sibling behavior" and that it would toughen Wally up. It was clear to Wendy that Walter did not approve of Wally's extra curricular activities. Walter thought Wally was a sissy.

Wendy never trusted Walter, and when she discovered his affair with a woman from work, it was all she could stand. The next day she found an attorney and filed for divorce. Walter was extremely competitive and was determined to win custody of *his* boys. The attorneys agreed on a custody evaluator to determine the best placement for the boys.

It was obvious in the evaluation that Walter secretly harbored resentment about Wally's choice of activities. It became even more evident that if the boys were placed with Walter, Winston's hockey lessons would continue, but Wally's acting and dance lessons would be cancelled.

The evaluation recommendations were strong. It was pointed out that Walter's favoritism created conflict between the boys. He neglected Wally, and their relationship was weak.

Wendy was supportive of both boys pursuits. Wally started taking karate lessons and grew stronger than Winston. Winston stopped bullying Wally. She had her hands full trying to juggle after school hockey, dance and karate lessons. But, Wendy treated the boys equally.

Walter continued to go to Winston's hockey games. Wally has grown indifferent to his father.

Walter learned not all children are created equally.

24

IF YOU WANT TO LOSE CUSTODY...
NEVER CHECK DETAILS

Never check the specific details of any order or agreement. Checking details and specifics is a hassle. It is in your best interest if you are late for all kinds of appointments and official dates. It is good to miss the school open house and to be late for your children's soccer games. This shows that you are an uncaring parent. Miss their music recital and their school play. Forget your children's pediatric appointments.

Create havoc in your child's life. Promise to pick them up after school and conveniently "forget." This is one of my favorites. Your child will be sitting out in front of the school with tears streaming down their face. The school resource officer or the principal will come out to see why they are there. Your child will tell them between sobs that obviously you have forgotten to pick them up. This strategy leaves quite an impression on school personnel.

When you are finally contacted by the principal or school resource officer, sound angry and bothered that they have called you. You can't act surprised like you have forgotten. That gets you sympathy and the benefit of the doubt. You don't want that. Make it a good show. Communicate that you have been inconvenienced and burdened.

Never offer the other parent the *Right of First Refusal*. The Right of First Refusal is where Parent A has to check with Parent B to see if they want to care for the child while Parent A goes out. This is used instead of Parent A getting a babysitter to watch the children or asking another family member. It is easy to conveniently forget that you were supposed to check with the other parent and simply drop your child off at their grandparent's house for the night while you go out. Just make sure that the other parent discovers you have done this.

Switching weekends with the other parent and then forgetting or claiming that you really didn't trade weekends also works under this category. Once you have gotten your weekend, claim the other parent agreed to forfeit their weekend.

Finally, make arrangements with the other parent to drop the children off at an important family event (like their grandmother's birthday party). Then, make sure you are out of town at that time. Claim you were confused about the date.

Doc Joe's Words of Wisdom
Some people say you shouldn't sweat the small stuff. If you are a good parent, you sweat everything, the big details and the small details, as well. Good parents make sure they know what their children are up to, what the travel arrangements are, and who will be supervising them. Good parents do not leave things to chance or make assumptions about their children's care or supervision.

It is wise to assume something bad is going to happen whenever you are making plans for your children. This does not mean that you should be paranoid, but if you assume that something could go wrong, you will incorporate things into your planning to make sure there are provisions in the event something does go wrong.

Make sure your child knows how to get in touch with you if they aren't picked up after school. If you aren't available or don't answer your phone, make sure they know how to get in touch with another family member or family friend who will assume a responsible role for them.

Security is the main concern when it comes to your children. Never assume the other parent will always follow through. Make sure you have made a safety plan for your children. Always follow through when you make plans with your child.

If you are making some type of arrangements or switches with the other parent, make sure you document it in writing. Never make an agreement with the other parent unless you have written down the changes in detail, and both of you have signed the document.

Yaz and Yvette

Yaz and Yvette were childhood sweethearts and married the same weekend they graduated from high school. Soon after marriage, Tamara was born.

Yaz and Yvette were both immature, and after divorcing they continued to bicker with each other. They were forever quarreling about who should have the child on the holidays, and they never seemed to be able to settle any disputes on their own. Their attorneys worked out an extremely detailed divorce decree that was very specific about where the child would be, and it included a *Right of First Refusal* clause.

Yaz soon found a new wife and became a house husband. His new wife had a small child, and Yaz devoted his days to caring for her child and keeping house. Yvette found a career she enjoyed.

One day when Tamara was sick at school, the nurse called Yvette and suggested that Tamara needed to be picked up. It was Yvette's week to have Tamara, and since she was working, she called her own mom to pick Tamara up from school and keep her for the day. Yvette's mom lived a half hour from Tamara's school. Yaz lived three minutes from the school.

Yvette neglected to consult her divorce decree. She wrongfully assumed that the *Right of First Refusal* clause was only for overnights. This was not the first time that Yvette used her mother to care for Tamara when she was sick.

Yaz became infuriated when he learned that Tamara had to wait at school for such a long time for her grandmother to pick her up when he was only a few minutes away. Yaz was tired of Yvette's defiance. She was constantly ignoring the details of their divorce agreement.

Yaz went to court and asked the judge for some sort of intervention. The judge ordered that Yaz is the only parent called when Tamara has any illness at school, and Yvette is required to consult Yaz before any outside caregiver is used.

Yvette discovered that ignoring details (refusing the Right of First Refusal) was a costly mistake.

The devil *is* in the details.

25
IF YOU WANT TO LOSE CUSTODY...
JOIN A CULT

Join a cult. It is one of the easiest ways to destroy your credibility and alienate your children. Cults come in many sizes, numbers and varying beliefs.

Join a cult that believes in extraterrestrial forms of life. These are people who believe that they have seen UFOs. Voicing these types of things in the middle of a custody battle will certainly effect the outcome.

Join a cult that believes in conspiracies. It can't be some run of the mill conspiracy like the Kennedy assassination or the bombing of Pearl Harbor. It will need to be more unique and include bizarre connections. This strategy requires some very creative thinking. Incorporate family and friends in the context of the conspiracy. Convince them to believe the same things you do. Or, convince them you are a nut. Either way brings an effective note to your conspiracy.

Devote excessive time to this strategy. Join a newly created religious sect. This also leaves a lasting impression on people. Dress in new and creative ways. Stop your personal hygiene and attract attention. Paint your house an objectionable color.

Become delusional and believe you are someone you are not. Begin to believe you are the reincarnated Buddha. This is bound to convince the judge you are too crazy to be taking care of children.

To lose your custody battle through this strategy, you need to be convincing. If you really want to be convincing, arrange to be interviewed on television or radio about your experiences. Tell a reporter that you have been abducted by space aliens and had sexual relations with one.

<u>Doc Joe's Words of Wisdom</u>
Good parents keep their behavior in check. Everyone is allowed to be a free spirit in the United States. You are allowed

to believe whatever you want as long as it doesn't infringe upon the rights of other people.

Good parents do not allow their behavior, or their resulting belief system to disrupt the lives of their children or bring undue attention to their children.

Grow up and behave yourself. Let your child grow up without your weirdness disrupting their lives.

Zane and Zoe

Zane and Zoe dated before they married. Zoe was overweight, and Zane was different. He was a bit of an oddball and lacked social skills in most settings. Their two children were a simple addition to their simple lives. But Zane and Zoe married young and when Zoe started at the community college, she began to realize that Zane didn't offer her the life that others had. She lost weight, studied and became more productive and secure. She quickly matured, and Zane stayed stagnant.

As typically happens when one spouse grows and the other does not, Zane and Zoe became distant. Zoe continued to study and graduated with an associates degree. She got a better job. Zane continued with his delivery job. He became resentful but refused to better himself. Zane's social withdrawal worsened, and the only people he associated with were the kids. One day, a coworker invited Zane to an after work meeting. His coworker told him it was a social gathering. Zane was angry with Zoe and knew it would bother her. It was his night to watch the kids, but he accepted the invitation anyway.

Zane felt welcomed at the meeting. Everyone talked to him and made him feel as if he were somebody. They shook his hand and didn't make him feel odd. He felt like one of them. He never really understood the purpose of the meeting. One guy got up and spoke to the group about tranquility. He didn't really know the meaning of the word, but the speaker made it sound interesting.

Zane continued to attend the meetings because it frustrated Zoe. It was on the same night as Zoe's evening class. He left it up to her to find a sitter for the kids. Zane never really understood the speakers even though they spoke about simple things like peace, love and quietness.

As Zane and Zoe grew more distant, Zoe planned her escape. She began to hide money away for an attorney. Zane grew more engrossed in his group meetings. He started doing odd things and began buying all white clothing. He would sit silently for an hour at a time telling Zoe that it was his meditation time. One night, Zane took the kids to his meeting. They came back telling Zoe they had a good time.

Zane had never placed the children in harm's way and had always been involved. He took their son to scout meetings and attended school functions. But, Zane had never really spoken with anyone due to his lack of social skills. Now, Zane began quoting odd literature to people and introduced himself to everyone. He told them about his inner peace. He spoke about the importance of love in the world.

Zane's involvement with the group deepened. He started following their suggestions on each component of his life. He was spouting their literature about life and love and how to raise your children. Zane checked with a member of the group about all decisions regarding his life.

A member of Zane's group was an attorney and handled his divorce. The attorney waged a negative battle and tried to paint Zoe as an unfit mother. Zoe's attorney was forced to fight an equally ugly battle and began to question Zane about his membership in the group. When Zoe's attorney used the word "cult" to describe the organization, Zane's attorney went wild and began shouting objections.

Before Zane's testimony about peace and love and inner wisdom was done, it was readily apparent that he was not the same person that Zoe had married. His monologue was vague and full of obviously memorized lines.

The judge was so dismayed by the lack of focus on Zane's part that he decided a psychological evaluation would be needed before Zane should spend any more time with his children.

Zane refused to be evaluated at the recommendation of his group.   As a result, Zane has no individual time with his children.

Be careful what you CULTivate.

Explanation of Terms

The following terms are commonly found in family court situations. The definitions are not definitive, nor are they considered to be legal terms. Each state has its own particular processes when it comes to how family legal matters are handled. Always check your state's unique proceedings and definitions.

ALIMONY - Alimony is money paid from one parent to another after or during a divorce. Alimony can be temporary or permanent. Sometimes there is "bridge the gap" alimony which is temporarily paid to one parent while they get back on their feet or train for a new or further career.

ATTORNEY - An Attorney is a professional who is licensed to practice law. A Family Law Attorney is an Attorney who has specialized training and specializes in practicing Family Law cases.

CASE MANAGEMENT – Case Management is a legal proceeding to assist the Judge in knowing the current standing of a court case. Minor or informal matters are often addressed in a case management conference. Sometimes case management conferences are used to determine when a trial will be scheduled.

CHILD SUPPORT - Child Support is money paid from one parent to the other during or after divorce to financially assist with raising the children. Child support is typically paid to a parent until the child or children reach the age of 18 or until the children graduate from high school.

CONTEMPT - Contempt is when a person is in direct violation of something the court has ordered. It can also be considered Contempt when someone is disrespectful to the judge or the court procedures.

COURT HEARING - A Court Hearing is like a trial, but usually not as formal or as long. A Court Hearing can be used to bring the Judge up to speed on your case, or have some minor matters (major matters are also sometimes addressed) addressed by the Judge. Matters addressed in Hearings are often temporary rather than permanent in nature. Hearings are often used to address matters after a divorce has been finalized. Usually both parties are required to attend a Hearing. Official testimony and evidence can be presented during a Hearing just like it can in a Trial.

COURT ORDER - A Court Order is an official document (proclamation) which is signed by a Judge which makes a specific statement or ruling. An Order is usually very specific and defines a relationship or what someone is supposed to do.

COURT TRIAL - A Court Trial is an official court proceeding that usually indicates final matters are being addressed and are being addressed for permanent purposes. A finalized divorce is usually done at a Trial instead of a Hearing because it is the final nature of a divorce.

CUSTODY FACTORS - The specific issues that a Judge must address and discuss in a final decree regarding the custody of children are referred to as Custody Factors. These can be specific or general in nature. Some factors address the relationship the parent has with the children while others address how likely a parent is to facilitate a relationship between the children and the other parent.

CUSTODY INVESTIGATION - A Custody Investigation is an official evaluation of a family during a divorce to determine the best placement for the children. It is often done by a psychologist and will include psychological testing, review of records, observations of all persons involved and extensive interviewing.

DEFENDANT - This is a legal term used for someone who is being charged with a crime or who has been sued. It is sometimes used to refer to someone who is testifying. It is rarely used in a family law case. It is often used in domestic violence cases.

DIVORCE - A legal proceeding that ends a marriage between two individuals.

DOMESTIC VIOLENCE INJUNCTION (DVI) - A Domestic Violence Injunction is a Court Order that instructs another person not to threaten you, commit violence against you or harass you. Sometimes DVIs also instruct other people to have no contact at all with you and also instructs the person not to communicate with you directly or through anyone else. DVIs also sometimes instruct another individual to stay away from your home and work and to stay a certain distance away from you at all times (500 feet is the usual distance).

EXPERT WITNESS - An Expert Witness is a professional who provides testimony in a court proceeding. There are different experts for each different field of profession. There can be family law experts, child custody experts and accounting experts to name but a few.

FATHER - A Father is a biological male who impregnated a woman who gave birth to a child. In some cases a man is considered the father if he has adopted the child or was the sperm donor.

GENERAL MAGISTRATE - A General Magistrate is a court official who assists Judges by conducting official court business like holding hearings and trials. In most cases the decisions of General Magistrates must be signed off on or approved of by a Judge prior to becoming final. Most General Magistrates were practicing attorneys before being elected or appointed to their positions.

HALF SIBLING - A child who has the same mother or father as another child but does not have both parents in common is referred to as a half sibling.

HEARSAY TESTIMONY - If someone attempts to give testimony about what someone else said, it is referred to as hearsay testimony and is typically not admissible. Under certain circumstances, some professionals are allowed to testify what was told to them by others. Most lay persons are not allowed to give this type of testimony in court.

INJUNCTION - An Injunction is an order from a court that requires a person, group, company or corporation to stop doing something.

JUDGE - A Judge is an elected or appointed individual who presides over the official business of the courtroom. Most often they have been to law school and were also practicing attorneys before they became Judges. Family court judges do not always have previous experience in family law.

LAWYER - See **ATTORNEY**

LITIGANT - Litigant is the term used to describe anyone involved in a lawsuit.

MAJORITY - Majority is reached when a person turns eighteen (18) years of age.

MARITAL SETTLEMENT AGREEMENT - A Marital Settlement Agreement is a legal agreement entered into by parents that addresses the issues of their divorce. Typically agreements are used to settle issues such as alimony, child support, asset and debt assignment and custody.

MEDIATION - Mediation is a formal process whereby the parties in a divorce attempt to reach an agreement to avoid litigation. Mediations can address all or partial issues of a divorce. The mediator's job is to facilitate the process and to make sure the negotiations are handled in a fair and balanced manner, free of coercion.

MEDIATION AGREEMENT - A Mediation Agreement is the official document outlining the results of the mediation. It may cover all issues of divorce or only some of the issues.

MINOR CHILD(REN) - Any person who has not yet reached the age of maturity (18 years of age).

MOTHER - A Mother is a biological female who gave birth to a child. In some cases a woman is considered the mother if she has adopted the child.

MOTION - A Motion is an official filing with the court whereby one party is asking the court for some type of action.

NO CONTACT ORDER - A No Contact Order is a Court Order that forbids one individual from having any type of contact with another individual even through third parties. Contact through third parties means that no information can be relayed through other people to the person who is protected. Third party contact is forbidden usually to avoid the possibility of threats or coercion.

PARAMOUR - Paramour is the term referring to a significant other (boyfriend or girlfriend) when a parent has not yet divorced from their current spouse.

PARENT COORDINATOR - A Parent Coordinator is typically a trained professional the court assigns to divorcing or separated parents in an attempt to teach them how to co-parent successfully. Parent Coordinators are often used to assist parents in reaching written agreements regarding the children on multiple matters. In some areas Parent Coordinators are given the authority to make non-substantial decisions for parents.

PARENT FACILITATOR - Parent Facilitator is another term for Parent Coordinator.

PARENTAL ALIENATION - Parental Alienation is any act or behavior by a parent that could potentially result in a child becoming alienated against the other parent. The act or behavior can be intentional or accidental. Parental alienation can be minor or severe and can be temporary or permanent.

PARENTING AGREEMENT - A Parenting Agreement is a document that lays out some written agreement between the parents. It is a contract that spells out whatever the parents have agreed to, or what the court has ordered for them.

PARENTING TIME - Parenting Time is a term used to describe the time children spend with each parent. It was formerly known as visitation.

PARTIES - In family court the term Parties typically refers to the Mother and Father. The children in the family are not referred to as Parties.

PLAINTIFF - In a family law case the Plaintiff is the person who initially filed the lawsuit (typically the divorce). They will be listed first on the case name. An example: John Smith versus Mary Smith (where John Smith would be the plaintiff).

POST-DISSOLUTION - This is a term that refers to any items or matters which occur after a divorce is finalized.

PRE-DISSOLUTION - This term is used to refer to any matters that are addressed or handled prior to the final divorce decree being issued.

PREVAILING PARTY - The Prevailing Party is the litigant in a lawsuit who wins the motion or trial. In family court the term prevailing party is rarely used because no one "wins" in family court.

PRIMARY PARENT - This term is used to refer to the parent with whom the children reside the majority of the time. It is becoming an antiquated term.

PROCEEDING - A Proceeding is any court meeting at which official business will be conducted. It may be referred to as a Hearing, a Trial, or a Case Management Conference.

PRO BONO - Pro Bono is when services are given to someone and no fee is charged for those services.

PRO SE - Pro Se is a term used to describe when someone is acting as their own attorney.

PSYCHIATRIST - A Psychiatrist is a medical doctor who has specialized training in mental and emotional disorders. Psychiatrists typically treat individuals through the use of medication.

PSYCHOLOGICAL EVALUATION - A Psychological Evaluation is an official evaluation conducted by a psychologist that typically includes psychological testing. The evaluation, which usually is presented in an official report, is a thorough interview including the entire life span development of a person. It usually includes information about a person's family of origin, their career history, and their educational path. The ultimate goal of a psychological evaluation is to determine any psychological or emotional issues faced by a person and to provide an accurate diagnosis of an individual. In family court, a psychological evaluation is often performed to determine if a parent is potentially detrimental to their children.

PSYCHOLOGIST - Psychologists are social scientists who have specialized training in a variety of areas including human development and behavior. They are able to diagnose mental, emotional and psychological disorders. In family law cases, they evaluate parents and children and are often called as expert witnesses to assist the court in making determinations about placement and other family issues. Most psychologists have an advanced doctoral degree.

RESPONDENT - In a family law case the Respondent is the person who is second in the lawsuit (typically the divorce). They will be listed second on the case name. An example: John Smith versus Mary Smith (where Mary Smith would be the respondent).

RESTRAINING ORDER (RO) - A Restraining Order (RO) is similar to a DVI in that it instructs another individual to stay away from you. It is typically used when someone has harassed, threatened or actually hurt someone else. The RO restricts the contact they can have with the individual who has obtained the Order.

RULING - A Ruling is the decision and also the reasons the court chose to act or decide the way it did.

SECONDARY PARENT - This term is used to refer to the parent with whom the children reside the minority of the time. It is becoming an antiquated term.

SEPARATION - Some states have a legal separation in which a document is filed with the court indicating that a married couple has now officially begun the process of divorce.

SOCIAL INVESTIGATION - A Social Investigation is an official evaluation of the family during a divorce to determine the best placement for the children, but it is not as extensive as a Custody Investigation. It does not typically include psychological testing. It does include observations, review of records, and interviews.

SOCIAL WORKER - Social Workers are employed and utilized to assist people in receiving social services. In some cases, social workers are used to assist the court in issues involving family matters. Different states have differing requirements to be called a social worker and some have bachelor's degrees while others have masters or doctoral degrees.

STEP CHILD - A Stepchild is the child of someone else to whom you marry. When a parent remarries or marries another person who has children, the children of the other parent are referred to as step children.

SUA SPONTE - Literally translated as "of one's own accord," in a family law case, Sua Sponte typically means that your judge has decided to order something on their own without either side filing a motion asking for the judge to rule on something.

VISITATION - Visitation is an outdated term used for the time children spend with each parent. It was typically used to describe the time the children spend with a secondary custodial parent.

<u>Notes</u>

<u>Notes</u>

<u>Notes</u>

<u>Notes</u>

<u>Notes</u>

Questions, thoughts or comments?
Please email Dr. Saturley at
DocSat@me.com